HOW I TRANSFORMED MY SON'S BASEBALL CAREER

BOBBY MINOR WITH GERMAN DURAN

CONTENTS

As a parent of a youth baseball player, it can be difficult to watch your child struggle. Hitting is often considered the most important aspect of baseball, and it can be discouraging to see your child fall behind their teammates. However, it's important to remember that everyone develops at their own pace. Just because your child isn't hitting as well as other players their age doesn't mean they won't find success on the baseball field. Every player has their own struggles, and it's up to the parents to help them through it. With time and patience, your child will develop into the baseball player they're meant to be.

We do everything we think we should to help them succeed, from shelling out thousands of dollars (not an exaggeration) on the latest bat technology and weekly hitting lessons, but it can be very frustrating when your son doesn't perform in games. Not to mention all the money you spend on organizational and travel costs. It adds up and all you want from your son is for him to play the way he's capable of.

I get it. I've been there, done that. A little over two years ago my then 14-year old son Julian was ready to give up on his dream and quit baseball.

MY SON WAS READY TO GIVE UP ON BASEBALL

It can be heartbreaking to see your son struggling with something he loves. As a parent, you want nothing more than for your child to be successful and happy. But sometimes, despite our best efforts, our children face difficulties and setbacks.

When your son is struggling with baseball, it can be tempting to give up. But as a parent, you know that baseball is more than just a game. It's an opportunity for your son to learn important life lessons. By teaching him how to persevere through difficult times, you're helping him to develop essential character traits that will serve him well throughout his life. Though it may be painful to watch your son struggle, remember that the lessons he learns now will stay with him long after the baseball season is over.

But I'm getting ahead of myself.

To fully understand our journey and appreciate where we are now I need to go back over 30 years ago to the birth of my first son, Caleb.

Caleb was born in August of '91 and was immediately exposed to the great game of baseball. Within a couple weeks of his birth he was already at the ballpark watching me play semi-pro baseball with the Fort Worth Lobos. By the age of two he had a sweet little left-handed swing and by three was playing tee-ball with 5 and 6 year-olds. While he wasn't the best player on his team he wasn't the worst either (somewhere in the middle) and held his own among the older kids. When he began playing with his own age group at 5, he was one of the best. By age 7 he looked like a mini "Will Clark", both batting and in the field. For Caleb it was "all baseball all the time" from the time he could hold a bat and take a swing. A couple of months before he turned 9 something changed. I say it as if it was a sudden event but in reality it most likely had been building for a while. We were a week into "A" All-Stars when Caleb decided he didn't want to play baseball any longer. Not sure exactly what happened but my best guess it was too much, too soon and I pushed him too hard from an early age. Crazy thing is he started playing junior golf where it's you against the course (no coaches) and thrived.

I HAD TO GET THIS RIGHT FOR HIM

I share that to say that with Julian I wanted to learn from my mistakes (Ah, the benefits of having a second child...) and introduce him to baseball early but let him go at his own pace. If the time came that he wanted to get serious about baseball I would be there to support him, but it wouldn't be the grind it was with Caleb.

He started playing when he was 6 and displayed a love for the game and a desire to get better almost from the beginning. Even still for the first couple of years he only played rec ball and didn't start playing select until he was 9. A friend of mine coached a 9U team and needed a 10th player and asked if Julian wanted to play. Julian had fun, made some new friends, and was pretty much the worst hitter on the team batting a minuscule .162 (6-37) in 33 games. I chalked it up to making the jump from rec to select. That fall they only played 8 games and he still brought up the rear batting .250, .167 lower than his next closest teammate. One bright spot was he did lead the team in walks and struck out less than he walked.

True to his nature Julian kept working hard and the following spring we actually started to see some improvement. In 37 games he batted .378 and was no longer bringing up the rear, he was now middle of the pack. If I'm being honest have to admit this was more fun.

The upward tick continued into the 11U fall and the following spring. On a side note, before 11U we had only played AA but moved up to AAA for 11U fall. By spring we would be playing Majors and stay there. What's interesting is that not only was he getting better, he was getting better while playing better competition. Things were looking up.

I WAS BEING WAY TOO HARD ON MY SON

Once we (and I say "we" because I coached the team...) moved up to 12U (both fall and spring) we had a lot of fun. As a team we had one of the better 12U Major teams in DFW (8 out of our 11 players from that team played varisty for their respective high school as sophomores...) and

Julian was playing well. One thing that was happening at the time that I didn't realize was I was being way harder on Julian than the other players (Remember my older son Caleb??). In hindsight, because I wanted to avoid the "Daddy Ball" label my standard for Julian was much higher than anyone else. On the outside he handled it well but I know it was hard for him. Every failure, no matter how big or how small, was a major issue. This caused him to become outcome focused instead of process focused and started to mess him up. The progress we had been seeing began to stall. I started to worry that Julian might follow the path of his older brother and quit baseball

but he kept playing. To avoid that happening I decided to not coach once we moved up to 13U that fall. We took most of our team to another organization and the team was coached by a former Major Leaguer. Maybe that was just what was needed because Julian hit .379 and actually had a tournament where he went 12-18 including 10-14 on Sunday where they went 5-0. He ended the fall on a high note and seemed to be having fun again.

#	Roster	GP	PA	AB	H	1B	2B	3B	HR	RBI	R	HBP	ROE	FC	CI	BB	SO	AVG	OBP	SLG	OPS
1	Julian Minor	17	38	29	11	10	1	0	0	8	5	2	1	1	0	7	5	.379	.526	.414	.940

He was excited about coming back in the spring. For me not coaching was an adjustment but I started getting used to only being a parent. My wife liked it too.

Little did we know at the time, but our coach would end up getting a corporate job with the organization and wouldn't be able to coach the team in the spring. They say that when one door closes another door opens and that's exactly what happened. Julian had the opportunity to play for another really good team with an awesome coach that was firm, but fair. We made the move very optimistic. Not sure exactly what was going on but Julian struggled to start the season.

Through 12 games he was only hitting .174 and had 12 strikeouts (leading the team) to only one walk. We had no idea what was going on. True to his nature he kept trying to work through it. He saw a video of one of his swings and realized he wasn't creating any separation when he loaded. He focused on trying to keep his hands back when his front foot hit the ground. In his next game it was more of the same. After his first two at-bats he was 0-2 with two more K's. In his third AB he was down in the count 0-2 when something happened. He kept his hands back and smoked the ball over the centerfielder's head for a stand-up triple. Starting with that triple he would go four for his next six with two triples, a double, a walk, and only one strikeout. He figured it out and he was on fire.

In their next tournament he was back at the top of the order batting leadoff. They were playing another good team with a big kid on the mound that could throw gas. The first pitch of the game was a fastball up and in that hit Julian on the hand. When it hit him he dropped the bat immediately and went down to the ground like he had been shot. You could tell he was in extreme pain. There was only one problem. The umpire said it hit his bat and not his hand and was a foul ball. His coach was livid. After five minutes of trying to convince the umpire to no avail, Julian finished the at-bat by lining out to the shortstop. In his next at-bat he lined a single to center, stole second, and scored on a base hit.

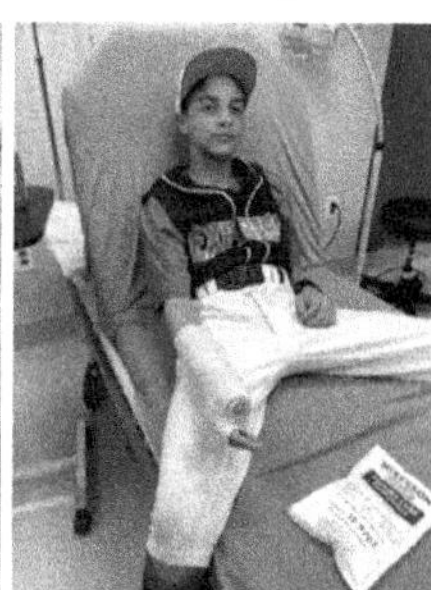

It then started to rain and we were in a delay. While we were in the car I told him to let me see his hand and his right thumb was twice the size of his left thumb and he couldn't move it. I told his coach we were leaving and we went straight to the ER. Turns out the umpire was wrong. Julian's right thumb was shattered and he was going to be out for 6-8 weeks. This pretty much meant his season was over right when he started to heat up.

Almost 8 weeks to the day he had his cast removed. The very next day we had a 6am flight to the Dominican Republic for an international baseball event. This should be fun. Oddly enough, after two months of no baseball he actually played well and went 5-12 in four games. We made it back home in enough time to go to Florida with his travel team for their season-ending World Series. Julian went a non-eventful 2-8 with a walk and was eager to get ready for the fall.

As much as I would love to tell you he lit it up in the fall, quite the opposite happened. He could never regain the momentum he was building before fracturing his thumb. In 25 games he hit a disappointing .158 (6-38) and led the team in strikeouts with 16 compared to only 9 walks. He finished the fall with a 7-game hitless streak. Not exactly how you want to go into the off-season.

For Julian there really isn't an "off-season" because he's always working and that's what he did, keep working. He also made the move to a new team with an organization with a great reputation for helping players thrive once they get to high school and then play at the next level.

We both had high hopes for his 14U spring/summer season. Unfortunately, instead of bouncing back from a less than stellar fall the downward trend continued. He finished his 32-game season with a brand new team and hit a whopping, wait for it, .200.

He had exactly 10 singles in 50 AB's (70 PA's). Not exactly the first impression you want to make on a new coach and new team. In his defense (pun intended) he did play lights out in the middle infield and only made 3 errors the entire summer.

	PA	AB	H	1B	2B	3B	HR	RBI	R	HBP	ROE	FC	CI	BB	SO	AVG	OBP	SLG	OPS
All Totals (32 games)	70	50	10	10	0	0	0	9	9	3	1	2	0	16	19	.200	.414	.200	.614

One bright spot is that he did walk a lot but there's a saying in the Dominican Republic, "You don't walk your way off the island," meaning you have to hit if you want to play at the next level. The same is true here. But sadly by the time the season ended he was virtually in tears after almost every game. Not because he was feeling sorry for himself but because he knew he was capable of so much more but couldn't get things to fall into place. On top of that even though we were finished with his travel ball season we still had to go to Ft. Meyers, Florida for a big Perfect Game event (the 14U Series Classic) that he got invited to. Yippee.

PG
THE SERIES
2019 14U PG SERIES CLASSIC
JUL 26 - AUG 1, 2019
JETBLUE PARK - FORT MYERS FL
CENTRAL - #6

JULIAN MINOR
SS 5-9 125 R/R
UPLOAD PHOTO
ALL TOURNAMENT TEAM
ALL TOURNAMENT TEAM (PITCHING)
CERTIFICATE | LIST

Luckily, the event wasn't a total flop and he actually hit the ball decently, at least in comparison to how he hit over the summer.

(On a side note he pitched 6 innings and only gave up one run on four hits, one walk, with 7 K's, and made the all-tournament team as a pitcher even though he rarely pitched back home! On offense he had five hits, still all singles, in 14 AB's so a glimmer of hope. At least enough to not want to quit quite yet.)

On the way back home he asked if he could pick up with someone and play that weekend because he wanted to see if he could build on what he did in Florida and end the summer on a positive note. I told him it sounded good and I posted on Facebook that he was looking to play that weekend.

Good news, bad news. The good news is a team reached out and said they could use him. The bad news is it was an 18U team and he was coming off a 14U summer where he almost hit under the "Mendoza Line" (Google it later if you don't know what I'm talking about...) against 14U pitching. Facing dudes with beards that drove themselves to the game should be, at the very least, interesting.

Long story short it was an uneventful weekend of baseball but there was one thing that happened off the field that would change the trajectory of his baseball career forever in ways we wouldn't know at that time.

There's a saying that you can't connect the dots looking forward but you can always connect them looking back, meaning that the things that happen today may not make sense at that moment but looking back we'll be able to see clearly how it all played a role in getting us to where we are today.

Well, I had one of those "moments" the Saturday morning of that tournament.

Julian was about to start his freshman year at RL Paschal High School in Fort Worth, Texas. We moved into the house we did specifically so he could go to Paschal because of the academics and because of the baseball program.

There happened to be a dad in the stands of the team Julian was about to play that was sitting on a Paschal Panthers stadium seat. I had no idea who he was nor who his son was. Assuming his son played baseball for Paschal I decided to introduce myself. He was super nice and it turned out he was also a teacher at the school and his son was starting his junior year at Paschal and pitched & played outfield on varsity.

We started talking about how the summer went for each of our son's and he mentioned that his son really didn't play much because he was focused on working out and getting better. I wasn't exactly sure what he meant by "working out" so I asked him who he was working out with hoping to gain some context. His response was, "German Duran, the guy that used to play for the Rangers."

What was interesting is that German also went to Paschal (Graduated in 2003 & was drafted by the Reds out of high school), then went to TCU & Weatherford College before being drafted by the Texas Rangers in the 6th round.

I knew who he was but hadn't heard his name in a few years. I decided to Google him and see what he was up to these days and maybe reach out and see about Julian coming in for a lesson.

Figured it couldn't hurt.

It took a little digging (German really didn't have much of a web presence) but I was finally able to find a phone number for German. I shot him a quick text telling him I had a 14-year old son that I wanted to bring in to work with him. What I didn't tell him was that Julian had been working with someone for the past year that he liked and was only open to "trying out" German to see what he thought.

We got it scheduled and later that week Julian went for his first lesson with German. It was August in Texas (Can someone say, "hot!?") and German worked his butt off. Because this was primarily for German to get to see Julian and get an idea of where he was ability-wise, and for Julian to get to know German and his style, there were lots of cuts but only minimal instruction. German said he liked what he saw and felt he could help Julian become a better hitter. In the car, Julian and I talked about his experience and he liked it enough to say he was willing to come back. It was at least a start.

We scheduled another lesson for the following week and came back. This time German began to make "tweaks" to Julian's swing. Nothing major, but you could definitely begin to see Julian hitting the ball harder and starting to build some confidence. I wanted to be encouraging to Julian but personally, I took it with a grain of salt because I've seen it before- he raked in the cages so this was nothing new. The real test would be how would he perform in games.

After Julian's third lesson with him, German said something to me that didn't fully register at that time (remember connecting the dots...?) but would become the catalyst for completely changing Julian as a hitter and what I believe can change your son as a hitter too.

This is what German said...

"I'm Going to Teach Julian How to Think Like a Major League Hitter..."

What that exactly meant I had no idea but we would start seeing results a lot sooner than I ever imagined.

After a couple of months of Julian continuing to work with German I had an "ah-ha" moment after one of his fall tournaments.

Keep in mind that in his entire summer season (32 games) he only had 10 hits and all of them were singles. In this one fall tournament (4 games), he went 5-11 with, get this, FOUR DOUBLES!! He actually had one game where he went 3-3 with three doubles! These weren't bloop doubles either, these were line drives in the gap.

Needless to say, we were both super excited and couldn't wait to tell German. We told him, he chuckled and then said, "Lol, just wait until it really starts to click. That's when you're really going to start seeing the results." Baseball was becoming fun again.

That November Julian was selected to play for the Puerto Rico 15U team in the "World Comes to the Palm Beaches" tournament in West Palm Beach, Florida. He got to play against Nicaragua, Canada, USA, and Venezuela.

A couple of months later in January of 2020, he was selected as one of 80 high school players from across the country to participate in the USA Baseball/MLB Dream Series in Tempe, Arizona at the Angels spring training facility and be trained for four days by guys like Ron Washington, Jerry Manuel, and Mike Scioscia.

Ok, I know what you're probably thinking right now and it's the same thing I was thinking: "What exactly was German teaching him that was making such a drastic difference in his in-game performance?? What did it mean to think like a Major League Hitter??"

Keep in mind that up to this point Julian had worked several different guys on his hitting in addition to working on something almost everyday with me. At least three of his instructors played in the MLB, two were former MiLB hitting instructors, one was the nephew of one of the most popular MLB hitting instructors ever, and while I didn't play professional baseball I played D1 baseball (before getting hurt), played in Mexico several times, coached high school baseball, coached major's level select baseball, started a successful select organization, I'm friends with a ton of current and former professional players, and ran an event in the Dominican Republic for four years with the son of an MLB Hall of Famer. My point is, all of this baseball experience and we still couldn't "fix" Julian.

Back to German. I asked the $1,000,000 question, "What exactly are you teaching Julian that has changed him as a hitter? His answer was simple yet profound.

He told me that while Julian did need some tweaking to his physical swing his problem was with his mindset and approach, the mental part of hitting a baseball.

That's what separated professional hitters from most amateurs.

That's why they were spending about 80% of their time together on mindset and approach and only 20% on swing mechanics.

He was teaching him things he learned from his own personal experience as a Major League hitter.

Things he learned through trial and error, things he learned from sitting in the dugout next to guys like Michael Young and Josh Hamilton picking their brains, things he learned as a student of the game and a student of hitting.

He was teaching Julian to "think like a Major League Hitter."

Fast forward to the following summer, Julian's 15U summer.

Another new team & new coach but this time a totally different result.

Julian was a completely different hitter.

In 28 games he had 29 hits which included 7 doubles! He finished the summer batting .446/.589/.554 with a 1.143 OPS and was selected Five Tool POG and/or Notable Hitter multiple times.

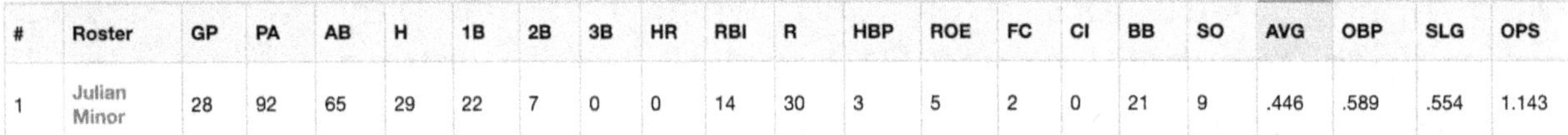

#	Roster	GP	PA	AB	H	1B	2B	3B	HR	RBI	R	HBP	ROE	FC	CI	BB	SO	AVG	OBP	SLG	OPS
1	Julian Minor	28	92	65	29	22	7	0	0	14	30	3	5	2	0	21	9	.446	.589	.554	1.143

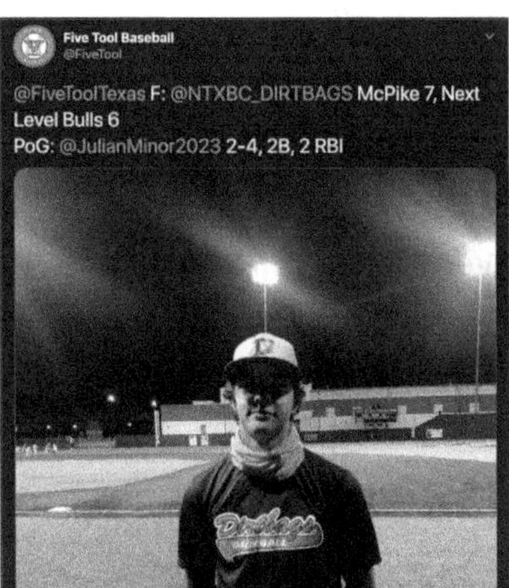

He was even selected "Honorable Mention" on Five Tool's "All-Summer Team". He still walked a bunch but now it was because he now had an approach at the plate and was looking for certain pitches in certain situations rather than being afraid to swing.

To finish off the Summer he went to the Dominican Republic to play for a week and was selected team MVP. As a bonus he also got to work some one-on-one with Jose Cano, Robinson's dad.

Once we got the fall he just kept hitting and getting on base. Another solid slash line in 12 games, .444/.500/.667, and

an even higher OPS of 1.167. He added a couple of triples to the mix as well to go along with four more doubles.

#	Roster	GP	PA	AB	H	1B	2B	3B	HR	RBI	R	HBP	ROE	FC	CI	BB	SO	AVG	OBP	SLG	OPS
1	Julian Minor	12	42	36	16	10	4	2	0	13	14	1	3	0	0	4	6	.444	.500	.667	1.167

This wasn't just a "phase", he was truly a different hitter primarily because German taught him how to think like a Major League Hitter and have an approach on every pitch of every at-bat.

In 40 games (summer & fall combined) he had 45 hits which included 11 doubles & 2 triples! He also walked 25 times and got hit 4 times. He reached base by hit or walk 70 times...CRAZY!

Jump to spring 2021, Julian's sophomore season of high school baseball. On a really solid 6A team with 13 seniors that would eventually lose to perennial powerhouse Southlake Carroll in the playoffs, he was one of two sophomores to make varsity and started 32 out of 34 games. He was also selected 3-6A All-District 2nd Baseman Honorable Mention. He split time between 2nd, SS, and DH and batted either 2nd or 5th. There's another saying in baseball, "If you hit, you don't sit." His glove has always been good but Julian stayed in the lineup because he could hit. (Not sure I would have thought I would ever be saying that.)

Another thing started to happen. He started hitting bombs during on-field BP... frequently. I mean hitting tanks. And

then that summer it finally happened in a game, not once, but twice in the same week. These weren't wall scrapers either, these were nukes. But they were also totally different

and only possible because of his approach in each situation. He continued to rake and had a solid 16U Summer/17U Fall season.

Julian also made another trip to the Dominican and trained for four days with some former major leaguers in San Pedro de Macoris at the stadium that hosts the Estrellas Orientales (Eastern Stars) and got to face some 90+ velo.

Fast forward to his junior year of high school. Julian started 31 out of 31 games at short and batted clean-up for a majority of the season. He ended up batting .321 with a .474 OBP, 1 HR, 22 runs, 17 RBI's, led the team in steals, and was selected 3-6A 2nd Team All-District Shortstop behind a senior that's a Texas Tech commit, in a district stacked with good shortstops. He even got a line drive single off of a current MLB pitcher (Hoby Milner) in their alumni game. Can't wait to see what the future holds.

Here's the reality. Meeting and working with former Texas Ranger German Duran over the past 3+ years has transformed Julian as a hitter and a player in more ways than I could ever imagine. It has taken him from a player on the verge of giving up the game he loves so much to a legitimate D1

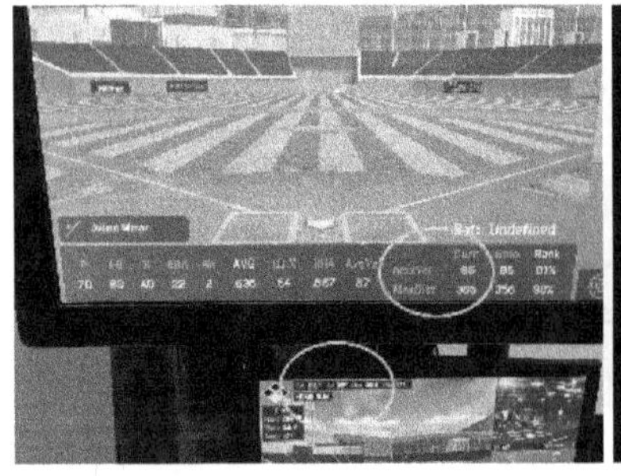

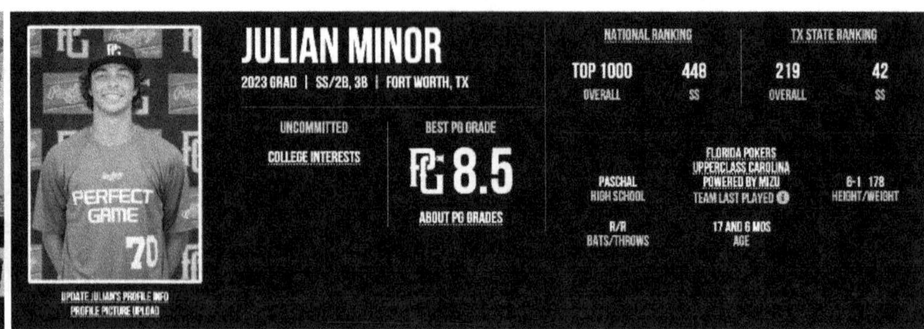

prospect and potential draft pick out of high school. There is no hype or fluff in what I just said, it's 100% true. But the reason has very little to do with mechanics or swing changes and everything to do with a new mental approach and how Julian now thinks.

This is different than anything Julian had experienced before. That connection, and what has happened since then, is the foundation for this book. Lol, I'm starting to understand what it means to "think like a Major League hitter."

They spend about 80% of their time together working on Julian's mindset and approach the exact same way German worked on his when he played in the MLB.

To be clear to fully capture what it means to "think like a Major League hitter" would take a series of books. What I've done in this book is take three core concepts that German has taught Julian that are the easiest to apply and will produce results the fastest. To be clear, these aren't "band-aids" or "quick-fixes", but are very real mindset and approach shifts that can and will change your son as a hitter if embraced and applied.

How long it takes is up to your son. Will he "buy-in" completely? Will he commit to working on making changes no matter how difficult things are during the process? Those are questions only your son can answer.

My promise to you is to give you three very real, tangible take-aways with no fluff and no filler. I'm focusing on quality rather than quantity. I'm giving you meat and nothing else. Time to eat.

I want to start with the one thing that I believe can have the biggest impact on your son's ability to hit at the highest level. This is something that by changing this one thing can transform your son as a hitter in a matter of minutes. This is most likely why he is a beast in the cages and BP and struggles and is inconsistent in games. This was the first thing German taught Julian.

It was their second or third time working together and German was throwing live BP to Julian. Almost every single one was a barrel resulting in a line drive. German then started doing this drill with Julian where he took 10 balls and told him he was going to give him two rounds of five where he would throw a 2-seam, 4-seam, change-up, slider, and curve in no particular order. Julian's job was to only swing at the slider and take the other four pitches. Julian was swinging at the correct pitch but fouled them off each time. After 40 or so pitches German stopped and called Julian over. He asked Julian if he noticed the difference between when he was swinging at everything versus only swinging at sliders. Julian said when he wasn't looking for a certain pitch he was driving everything but when he was only looking for sliders he was just missing. German asked him if he knew why that was happening and he didn't. This is when German shared the first of many things that would change Julian as a hitter. He told Julian that the biggest mistake he was making as a hitter was he had "a passive mindset versus having an aggressive mindset."

What exactly does this mean? Think about this. What is your son's mindset when he's in the cages? If he is like a majority of hitters it's something like this, "I'm swinging at every ball unless I see it's an un-hittable pitch."It means that he has an aggressive mindset. He's in attack mode until he sees a ball is un-hittable and then he takes. What about in games? If he's like a lot of non-professional hitters that struggle his mindset is most likely like this, "I'm going to wait until I see if the pitch is good before committing to swing." That's exactly what Julian was doing when he was only supposed to swing at sliders. He was waiting until he saw it was a was a slider before deciding to swing. A lot of struggling hitters wait until they see a pitch is a strike before deciding to swing. It's the same thing. They wait until it's too late.

Now he may not be consciously thinking this but this is what his subconscious is telling his mind. This is a passive mindset. It means he's taking a "wait and see" approach to hitting. The problem is, if he's waiting to decide if he's going to swing, it's too late. You have to have the mindset that you are always swinging and you just shut down the swing if you don't like what we see. So if you don't have to decide if we are swinging, the only choice or decision to make is when do you start.

Depending on the distance and velocity he's facing he has less than half of a second (0.45 on average) to do the following things:
Determine the type of pitch...
Determine the speed of the ball...

Determine if it's a strike or ball (location)...
Load, stride, and get his front foot down...
Get the bat to the ball.

That's a lot that has to happen in a very short amount of time. If he's waiting to see 1-3 before deciding if he's going to swing, there's not much time if any, for 4 & 5 to happen on time and consistently. Will he still get some hits? Of course. Will he ever hit the way he's capable of ? Doubtful.

Does any of that sound like your son? If the answer is yes, there's hope. He simply needs to have the same mindset in games that he has in the cages. Sounds easy enough, right?

In all seriousness, that's exactly what he needs to do. The question is, how does he do it?

In the Dominican Republic (and other Caribbean countries) there's a saying, "You don't walk your way off the island." If you are a position player you have to hit to get signed (The exception to this would be a glove-first MIF or super fast CF). That's it point blank. Because of that you will see Dominican players swinging at everything that even sniffs the strike zone. They go up to bat with an aggressive mindset looking to do damage any pitch they can get the barrel on. They approach every at-bat like their lives depend on it because for many of them it does.

Right now, during every game at-bat, the little voice inside of his head is saying, "Wait, wait, wait, and then either ok or no." His subconscious is telling his brain to, "Wait until you see the pitch before deciding to swing. If you think it's good, ok, if not, then no."

What the little voice needs to tell him in games is the same thing it says in the cage, "Yes, yes, yes or yes, yes, no." From the second the pitcher begins his motion the batter is planning on doing damage to the ball and acts/reacts accordingly until he sees it's not his pitch.

A super simple thought to have is this, "Go until no." You are going to swing until you're not. The negative alternative is this, "If you wait, you'll be late." The one and only purpose of all this is to be on time.

Keep in mind the pitcher's #1 goal is to disrupt your timing, not strike you out. If he can throw off your timing even a fraction of a second that might turn that barrel into a rollover or popup.

Timing is really dancing with the pitcher because you must react to his movements. A hitter must put himself in the right position at the right time.

Early timing is better than late timing. If a hitter starts a little too early, he can always slow down and be right on any pitch he recognizes correctly.

On the other hand, if a hitter starts too late he cannot make up lost time and will probably rush or jump at the ball.

Once in motion, the hitter's eyes will tell him when and where to deliver the bat. If the hitter starts his ready motion late, he cuts down the time his eyes have to make a good judgment on where and when to deliver the bat and ends up using a very rushed movement.

To time a pitcher, a hitter must trust his eyes, know, and feel what he's looking at when he steps into the batter's box. After a pitch or two, a hitter should know if he's close to being on time or if he's too late or too early. It does not matter what pitch the pitcher throws because a hitter must always be on time for the pitcher's fastball. Once the ball is released, a hitter who is on time for the pitcher's fastball can make an adjustment to an off-speed pitch by simply slowing down for a split second and letting the ball travel to the hitting zone somewhere over the plate.

For a hitter, good rhythm and timing require moving in relation to the pitcher's motions. Most of the time, you want to start moving when the pitcher breaks his hands. Whether the pitcher works from the windup or the stretch, he will have to break his hands. He can't fool you. What you're doing is dancing with the pitcher.

When the pitcher breaks his hands, the hitter must maintain his posture and stride on time, landing on the inside of the balls of his feet. The front foot can land open, at almost a 45-degree angle. A hitter should not land on his heels.

Good hitters start early and slow while maintaining a fluid motion. Keep the motion going until your stride foot lands on the ground. You cannot get aggressive until your foot lands. Many hitters try to get aggressive before they land, turning their approach into a jump or lunge.

Starting your motion early is better than starting large. When a hitter starts early, it's much easier for him to adjust. A hitter can always slow down. A hitter who starts late can never catch up. If you start your motion too early, just say to yourself, "oh no, this is too soon," and slow everything down to a fluid movement. Don't stop. If you stop, you'll have to restart.

Hitters who chased bad pitches were often told to see the ball first, and then react. This old teaching doesn't work. The big problem with this idea is that the hitter will run out of time. The four-tenths of a second the hitter has to make a good decision will be gone.

Seeing the ball is a good idea, the hitter must see the ball while he's in motion or while he's getting ready to attack. The hitter starting early means

that the hitter's body is in motion and is set up to hit the pitch before the pitcher gets to his release point.
Don't be afraid of movement. Timing requires movement. The swing requires movement. Everything about hitting consists of good, fluid movements.
Remember this, if we're late on the fastball, or worse, when we freeze up on one, it's usually because we're simply not ready to hit.
In other words, the finger is not on the trigger.
To have a chance at hitting a 90+ mph fastball (or 60+, or 70+ depending on age), you have to assume that the next pitch is going to be a strike.
Every pitch, you're assuming you're going to get a good pitch to hit and you're going to take a controlled violent swing to achieve hard contact and good spin and flight.
If you're thinking, "I'm going to see if it's a strike first before I swing", it's too late. The ball will beat you.
The mentality is always, "Yes, yes, yes, Go!" on a strike...
...and "Yes, yes, yes, No!" on a ball.
You're never taking a pitch off. The switch is always on. The finger is always on the trigger.
Not "if" it's a strike. It's going to "be" a strike.
Take the "if" out of your mentality.

There's one drill German likes to do with Julian that you can do today that I like to call "The Vlad Sr Drill."

If you've ever seen Vlad Guerrero Sr at-bat then you'll understand the name of this drill. He was going to swing at anything and everything unless it was in the dirt. (Oh wait, he could hit those pitches too.) He was the poster boy for having an aggressive mindset. He also batted .318 over his 16-yr Major League career with over 2,500 hits. This is a drill that is most effective after you're good & loose and feeling good about your swing. This is designed to simulate game at-bats as best as you can without actual live AB's at game speed. Go through your normal progression whatever that may be. For many it will be something like this: tee, flips, then live BP. Then, you're going to do two things. First, have whoever is pitching to you move the L-screen as close to the plate as necessary to be able to throw strikes at about 80% of the speed you'll face in a game (TIP: Set up the L-screen 20 feet from the plate. Throwing 30 mph you will easily be at a reaction time of a 90 mph fastball. Throwing 25 mph will get you to 75 mph...). Second, prepare your mind for 100% focus and approach this like you're in a game. Do not rush this or cut corners. Pick a situation for every at-bat (runner on 2nd, 1 out, down by one in the bottom of the 5th, etc...) and go through your normal routine. Do this for four at-bats simulating game situations. Challenge yourself to have an aggressive mindset. Be aware of the situation before you step into the box and then it's "Go until no." You are going to "dance with the pitcher" and commit to swinging from the beginning up to the point that you see the pitch isn't hittable. During this drill you need to swing at pretty much everything unless it's un-hittable. This is different than a hit and run where you're trying to still protect the runner on pitches out of the zone. The point of this is to get you really aggressive with your mindset. You should want to hit every single pitch and you are going to swing no matter what. The reason for almost being too aggressive during this drill is because during games your default will be to go back to what you know, waiting to see the pitch before committing. It is way easier to throttle back from being too aggressive than it is to turn it up when you're not being aggressive enough. Do this as often as you can until you see your mindset begin to change. For some hitters they see a change almost immediately, for others it takes a little longer.

Once Julian focused on his mindset and started thinking "go until no", we began to see a big difference but there were still times times when his timing looked off. He wasn't waiting to see the pitch before deciding to swing like he used to but he was either way out front or getting gassed up on average fastballs. German asked him what pitch he was looking for in a certain count. When he was up in the count, down in the count, first pitch, with two strikes, etc. Julian's response was, "it depends." So German asked Julian to tell him more. Julian went on to explain that he was basically trying to outthink the pitcher and guess what pitch he was going to throw. This was sometimes based on what the pitcher had shown, ie, starting every batter off with with a fastball down the middle, or throwing a curve with two strikes. Lots of times it wasn't based on anything other than Julian's gut feeling. This explains why sometimes Julian would drive the ball (he would guess correct), sometimes be early (guessed fastball but got off-speed), and sometimes get gassed up (thinking off-speed but got fastball). After Julian explained this German he told him that the second mistake he was making that was keeping him from his full potential was he was guessing at pitches and thinking off-speed when he should be thinking fastball. He had Julian go

back and think about the 10-ball drill they do where Julian would focus on only one pitch.
In that drill Julian started focusing on having an aggressive mindset and was reading the pitch while he was in motion, and focusing only on one pitch, he was having better results. Julian had a tournament coming up and he wanted Julian to only swing at fastballs regardless of the count or situation. He said go up there and hunt fastballs. If you take a strike three that's not a fastball don't worry about it. Trust me during this process. Once Julian stopped guessing and started to only look for fastballs 95% of the time he became a beast. All he had to do was make sure to be on time. Baseball legend Ted Williams says this, "You have to hit the fastball to play in the big leagues."

Everything German does with Julian builds on the other things they work on. So if the first key is to have an aggressive mindset then right after that would be to stop guessing pitches and to think fastball and be on time.
First off, if you want to be a good hitter, you have to be great at hitting the fastball, period. If you struggle with the fastball, your approach and mechanics will fall apart the moment pitchers start establishing the fastball on the inner half of the plate while following up with the soft offspeed away. Mentally we can help our mechanics by thinking oppo gap - I'm taking every FB the other way - no matter where it is. By never getting off the FB timing wise and thinking I'm taking every FB the other way (even the inside FB), then the hitter will have a chance to be on the off speed pitch.
Here's what a couple of guys that know a thing or two about hitting have to say about this:

Andrew McCutchen on hitting a curveball: "They always say that the way to hit a curveball is to hit the fastball. If you're ready to hit the fastball, you can hit anything. As long as you're set, your base is good, you can adjust to the off speed."

Josh Hamilton on whether he ever looks for a breaking ball, "I never look for a breaking ball. I can't think about anything else besides the fastball. Just like everything with hitting, if your timing is good, it doesn't really matter what they are throwing."

Good timing means getting the body into a strong position so that when the stride foot lands, the ball is still far enough away. This allows the hitter to take his best swing at any pitch, at any velocity. A good hitter times the pitch, putting his body in the right place at the right time.

Timing and rhythm are crucial. You must be in a good balanced position to hit while the pitch is still far enough away for you to recognize it. Whatever kind of trigger you use: tap, kick, or stride. You have to start it early enough to give yourself as much time as possible to see the pitch. You must land on the balls of your feet at the correct time - when the ball is still about halfway to home plate - to give yourself as much time as possible to recognize the pitch.

When a hitter takes his stride and his front foot lands on the ground, the ball should be halfway between the mound and home plate or just a little past halfway. The problem is the hitter can't tell exactly where the halfway point is, but he does know that the ball isn't on top of him and he does know the pitcher doesn't still have the ball in his hand. The ball is moving toward home plate. Now all the hitter has to do is recognize the pitch and begin a good, aggressive swing.

A hitter may not see the ball correctly if he's late or feels everything is rushed. When hitters learn that timing is just putting the body in the right place at the right time, the ball will look bigger and the pitch will seem slower.

You cannot increase bat speed or swing harder to catch up to a fastball. Your bat speed is not going to change from pitch to pitch. What you can change, however, is your timing. When facing a hard thrower, don't try to swing harder. Start your rhythm and timing sooner and the bat will have a chance to get to the ball on time. Begin a motion that will set up your swing. It doesn't mean you should commit early by bringing the bat head around or start the swing itself early. You must get your front foot down before the swing begins and early motion allows you to separate to balance and be on time.

You've probably heard someone say, "Think fastball, react to off speed (or react curve)." While in and of itself it's not bad advice I would challenge you to only think like that with two strikes if you think it at all. The reason being you will be more apt to swing at a pitch outside of the zone and chase a pitch in a hitter's count. Ideally your up count swings to need be aggressive on fastballs middle-middle to middle-away. You should be able to react to the fastball in without looking for it or thinking about it. Think oppo gap on middle-middle to middle-away and turn and burn on the inside pitch.

Learning to recognize the pitch comes from practice and experience. The more pitches a hitter sees, the better chance he has of recognizing a pitch

correctly. The pitcher's job is to make it difficult for the hitter to recognize pitches by changing speeds, using deception and changing his timing.
After the ball is thrown, early recognition is the most important factor in hitting. You can't hit what you don't see. You should hit what you see-not what is thrown. The eyes will provide the information your body needs.
On the average, a thrown baseball takes about 4/10 of a second to reach the contact area. A hitter will use half of that time to recognize what the pitch is and the other half to deliver the head of the bat to the ball.
Coaches tend to pass over this point and go straight to the mechanics of the swing... timing-recognition and a strong mental approach are more important than the swing itself. The more pitches a hitter can see the better his chances are of being on time. Having two eyes on the pitcher and being balanced will help to develop these skills.
Recognizing the pitch while in motion leads to better timing and better decisions.
Your separation-reach (load) has movement. The swing has movement. You have to think strike. You can't wait to see the ball and then react. When a hitter guesses, he sits on a certain pitch but still swings to any other pitch. A hitter that anticipates a fastball has timing for a fastball but can still drive a bad or hanging breaking ball.
You can't be afraid of movement. Moving in a slow rhythm is more efficient than jumping or lunging at the ball. The head does move during separation and again during the swing. These movements are fine as long as the hitter maintains his posture. Because of the time factor the hitter has to see and recognize the pitch while he is getting ready.
While on deck - time the pitcher, see what he is throwing - ahead - even - behind in the count - with runners in scoring position - etc.
In the box - keep your eyes and head stable with both eyes on the pitcher - eyes level - parallel to the ground
Get into early rhythm.
Clear your mind of all outside thoughts. It doesn't matter if the bases are loaded in the bottom of the 9th. A hitter must be able to clear his mind and recognize correctly. This pitch - this moment - has to be part of your plan
Recognition leads to better strike zone management - better decisions - better counts to hit in -better situational hitters - deep counts - etc.
Here are three things to remember to help you always be on time on the fastball. First, have a good soft to hard focus. Loose muscles are quick muscles. Loose muscles around the eyes avoid eye-strain. Have a soft gaze with a broad focus on the pitcher during the wind-up, then a hard focus

transition to the pitcher's release point will give you early release point pitch recognition.

Second, have slow feet & a quiet head. Wanna make a 88 mph fastball look like 95 mph? Speed your feet up and increase your head movement. Wanna make an 88 mph fastball look like 82 or 83 mph? Slow your feet down and keep your head quiet. If the head moves, the eyes move. The more the eyes more, the faster the ball will appear.

And last but not least, anticipate before you react. Reacting is good because hitting is about letting go. But to show up on time, you anticipate. When you're sitting fastball while adjusting to off-speed, you're always anticipating a good pitch to hit. You're anticipating a strike. If you're sitting fastball you can't be surprised by the fastball. Remember to stay fastball ready and look away and react in.

One drill German does with Julian to help with being on time for the fastball is the short front-toss drill.

The short-distance front-toss hitting drill is fairly straight forward. As you shorten the distance between the release point and home plate, you're limiting the time the hitter has to react, mimicking high velocity in a controlled environment.

A good place to start is placing the L-Screen about half the distance of where you would normally place the L-Screen. (10-15 feet from home-plate).

The goal here is to have the feeder work both sides of the plate while the hitter focuses on initiating the swing in time while getting the foot down early enough. Once you're comfortable with your fastball timing have the feeder mix in some off speed by some exaggerated slower, higher flips but still only swing at fastballs.

Often times, a hitter gets beat by the fastball because the front foot lands too late.

Shorten the amount of time the hitter has to react to the pitch and then reinforce proper pre-swing movement.

The hitter should be able to make consistent contact by getting their bat to point of contact while initiating the swing earlier.

If you're chronically late, you have to start sooner.

If being passive rather than aggressive at the plate, and guessing at pitches were Julian's two biggest mistakes, then the third one was this, trying to cover the entire plate.

While in reality the strike zone and your hitting zone are both 3-dimensional, for the purpose of this think two-dimensional. I want you to focus on where the ball crosses the plate, first horizontally, then both horizontally and vertically. So we'll start with in and out then add up and down.

Think about this. Home plate is 17 inches wide, and while that might not seem like much it's approximately five baseballs wide. It's the same for everyone from tee-ball to the MLB. You can number those balls 1-5. This represents the five different horizontal locations the ball can cross the plate and that you have to cover. Picture it like this:

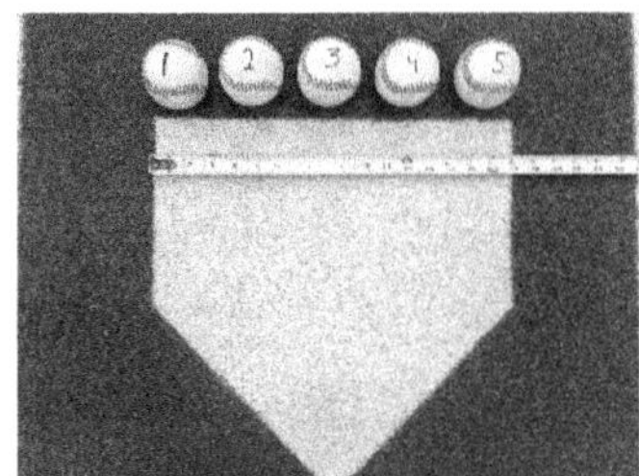

After getting a visual for these five different horizontal pitch locations, I want you to think about this. Even if you are only thinking fastball, trying to effectively and consistently drive a pitch that crosses the plate anywhere 1-5 is difficult, even for a professional hitter. That's why you shouldn't. I will even go as far to say not even with two strikes and I'll tell you why shortly.

The key for most hitters is to only look for pitches in the 2, 3, or 4 zones when in hitter's counts (0-0, 1-0, 2-0, 3-0, 2-1, 3-1, & even 1-1 at times). Meaning that you shouldn't swing at pitches that are in the 1 zone or in the 5 zone at all. Eliminate those zones entirely. (NOTE: Players with a more advanced approach can shift their "zone" depending on where their sweet spot is.)

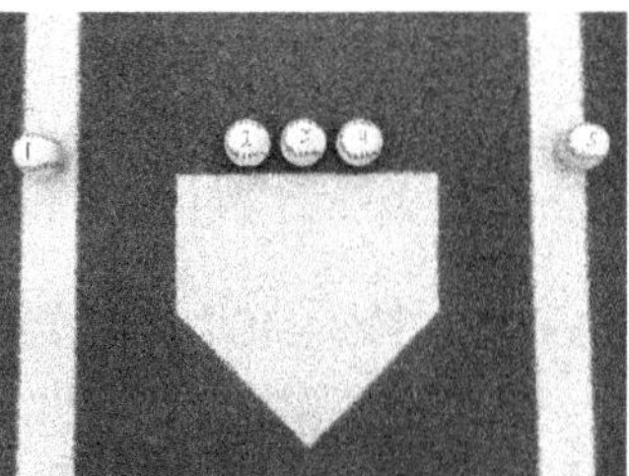

If you take both ball number 1 and ball number 5 out of the picture, you're left with the three balls that make up the middle of the plate:

Middle-middle is where you want to live most of the time. If you are able to utilize this approach properly, you are only going to swing at pitches that cross the plate where ball 2, 3, or 4 are (with 3 being true middle-middle). These are the pitches that you are on 100% focused on.

If you are locked in on swinging at these 3 middle zone locations (2, 3 & 4) then you are going to be much less likely to swing at pitches that are off of the plate, whether they are inside or outside. By focusing on those 3 balls right down the middle, pitches that are close, yet off of the corners will appear miles away (6″+) from your point of focus. Very often, the pitches that look like they are a 1 or a 5, are pitches that end up off of the plate when they pass through the hitting zone.

When you work this approach early in counts it helps you lock in on pitches you can drive. If you take some strikes that are 5's or 1's that's not a big deal. You want to swing only at the pitches that have a high percentage of being hard hit balls.

The pitches located in that 1 or 5 horizontal zone are most often pitcher's pitches, and will come with very slim odds of being hard hit regardless of the count. If you do swing at those pitcher's pitches early in counts then you are very likely to rollover or make weak contact. When you do this, you are only helping the pitcher out.

Remember, by taking the balls on the corners (low % hard hit) you are less likely to swing at pitches off of the plate and chase, driving up a pitcher's pitch count.

Just looking strictly at the numbers, pitchers generally only hit their spots on the corners (1 & 5) less than 10% of the time.

Even if it was a 10% chance for both corners, that means that 80% of the time you will either see a pitch in the meat of the plate (2, 3 & 4), or we will see 4 balls. If the pitcher does happen to hit the corner twice in an at bat, the odds show that it is highly unlikely to happen again.

By making zones 2, 3, and 4 your main focus, it also removes the element of "surprise" that many hitters face when they see a pitch directly down the middle.

If you are expecting to see it down the middle, and that's where your focus is, this cognitive trigger will nearly pull itself when the time comes.

With advanced hitters there is also an element of individual hitters handling certain pitch locations better than others. Some guys are great pull hitters and prefer the ball in, while other love the ball away.

You can still use this approach but don't be afraid to vary the horizontal locations that you are looking for.

If you are a big power guy the hammers the ball on the inner half then you can lock in on the horizontal locations of balls 1, 2, & 3 (RH hitter).

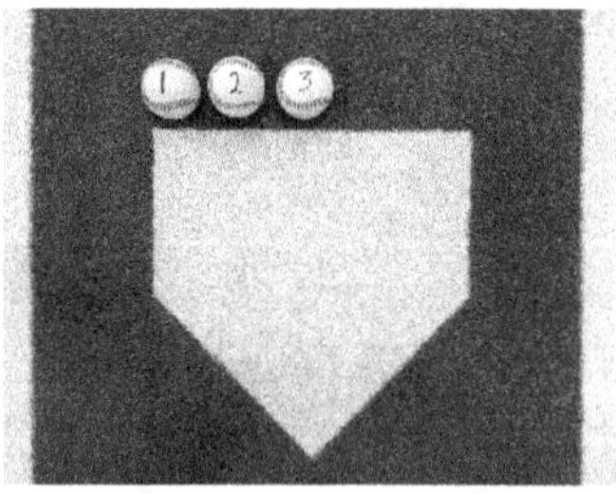

Likewise, if you are a guy that is great at driving the ball the other way and loves the ball on the outer half you might want to vary your one zone as well. This type of hitter might choose to lock in on balls in horizontal zones 3, 4, & 5 (RH hitter).

The caution with an approach that's not middle-middle is there is a greater possibility of swinging at those pitcher's pitches early in counts. This happens because balls in the 1 or 5 zone can very easily end up off of the plate.

What you are doing is starting to make yourself aware of having an approach at the plate, and actually understanding how to key in on one zone. The visual of looking for pitches in a specific zone creates a heightened sense of awareness when you get into the batters box.

It is also important to touch on the idea that you might be tempted to look for specific pitch types also (fastball, curveball, change-ups etc...). Like we talked about in the second chapter, you want to be locked in on the fastball with less than two strikes. With zero strikes, the overwhelming likelihood is that you will see a fastball (age and ability level obviously impact this a lot). At the highest level, guys can throw any pitch in any count, but in youth baseball, high-school, and even most college ball, sitting fastball is going to be the best approach.

Now, it is also important to make sure that you know you have to alter your approach slightly once you get to two strikes. When there are two strikes on a hitter they must expand their zone a little bit more and protect against those pitches that are in line with the 1 and the 5, and maybe even pitches that are off of the plate a bit (again this depends to an extent on the age/level of play).

If you're going to do anything I would say widen your stance some and choke up a bit but that's it. You've probably also heard to expand your strike zone with 2 strikes - I DON'T THINK SO! Professional hitters are taught to work off 3 balls in the middle and look 1 ball off center, so when we look away, just look 1 ball. You will be able to handle 6 more inches away easy and that will cover the plate but if you start looking on the corner (the black) you will chase balls off the plate. So be careful how you approach strike zone management.

At the lower levels, teaching plate discipline is even more important, but umpires are going to have a much bigger zone and you would much prefer that hitters are aggressive rather than passive. As players start to play at higher and higher levels, working with them to consciously develop better and better plate discipline through a measured approach is vital to their success.

Another one zone approach against guys throwing gas is to simply "cut the plate in half."

Facing high velocity will cause you to struggle with your timing and you might want shrink your "one zone" as much as possible.

In other words, in order to be on time, you have to "cheat" by focusing on one small location, especially on pitches middle in.

Though this makes you susceptible to off-speed or pitches away, it's an adjustment worth taking especially if the pitcher has established the fastball on the inner half of the plate.

If you're looking for a pitch middle-in, you're going to have to cheat and start sooner, so that means you'll have to take and not swing at anything on the outer half of the plate if you want to avoid being out front and hitting weak ground balls, pull-side.

On the other hand, if you're looking for a pitch middle-away, you're gonna half to sit back and let the ball travel a tick. This means any pitch middle-in, you're taking unless you want to get jammed.

When it comes to hitting fast pitching, every adjustment you make has a "give and take".

Sitting on off-speed leaves you susceptible to the fastball and vice versa.

The approach you choose will decide on the situation of the game, what pitches the pitcher has been throwing for strikes as well as how the pitcher is pitching your teammates.

How do you make the best choice? You watch the pitcher. This is how you develop your hitter's instinct.

This isn't "guess hitting." It's intelligent hitting and cutting the plate in half might help you make the best adjustment when you're facing a pitcher who's really pumping it on the mound.

REMEMBER THIS: Now let's look at a one zone approach incorporating both horizontal and vertical elements. The physical aspects of your swing are important, but we have to understand that the swing by itself will NOT stand alone. That's the point of this entire book and everything we are doing. A majority of the time, swing issues are a byproduct of not being on time and/or not having an approach at the plate.

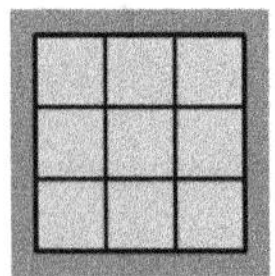

Here is another super simple approach that can be applied right away and will help immediately. I call it my Moneyball approach. You're going to lock in on one zone that's going to give you the greatest chance to do damage. When you do damage, that's money.

This expands on what we've already talked about with the five balls and horizontal plate coverage.

Start by visualizing the strike zone divided into to three rows of three squares which would make 9 total squares (see pic below). Within those 9 squares (the strike zone) we want to focus on particular "groups" of squares that will be your Moneyball zones. Having an idea of where you should be locked in on and which zones where you should not be locked in on is based on the count, who is on the mound, situation of the game, etc.

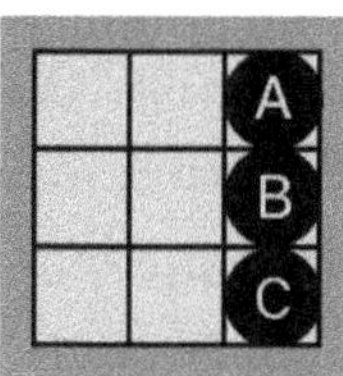

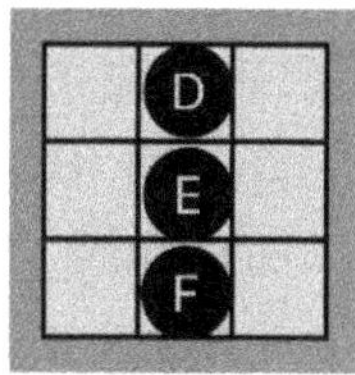

Boxes shaded green are in the strike zone. The areas shaded red are NOT strikes and are outside of the strike zone. If this is from behind the catcher then boxes A, B, & C are inside to a right handed batter and outside to a left handed batter. Boxes D, E, & F are inside to a left handed batter and outside to a right handed batter. Boxes G, H, & I are middle-middle for both lefty's and righty's.

To give a visual adding what we talked about earlier in this chapter we'll add five balls at the bottom for reference.

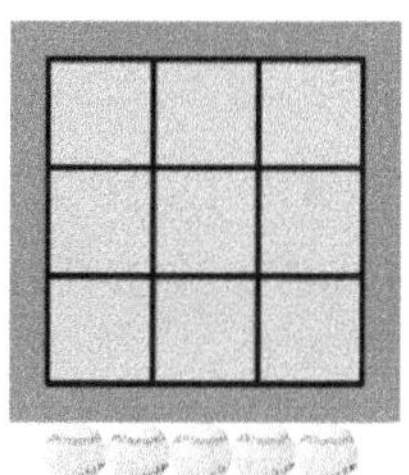

Every time you step into the batter's box you have to have an approach, a game plan. This means on every single pitch with no exceptions. As a hitter, you have to "lock in" on your Moneyball zone. You have to be looking for a specific pitch (usually a fastball) in a specific zone. This is your one zone.
This is based on 3 things:

Your strengths and weaknesses as a hitter...
The count and game situation...
The tendencies of the pitcher that you are facing...
Before I go into the specifics of the process, I want to explain the importance of being "honed in and zoned in" in the batter's box. One of my favorite quotes is this Michael Jordan quote, "Focus like a laser, not a flashlight." You may need to think about that quote for a few before it makes sense. But for a hitter, if you walk up to the plate looking for some pitch somewhere in the strike zone (not honed in; like using a flashlight rather than a laser), you will swing at pitches in the red all day long. (This also applies to seeing

the ball out of the pitcher's hand, but more on that some other time...) You won't have any plate discipline and you will chase all the pitches that the pitcher wants you to swing at. However, if you walk up to the plate with a focused, one zone plan that you trust, you won't chase pitches because you have ONE ZONE FOCUS. If something is not in your specific zone, your brain will alert you and tell you not to swing!

Hitters please understand that if you walk up to the plate with the mentality of "I'm looking for a strike somewhere in the zone," good luck dude! Baseball won't be fun for very long. That mentality might work up through high school, but if you have any aspirations of being a great hitter and playing at the highest levels, that can't be your mindset.

Ok, so what does the Moneyball approach look like?

Instead of solely focusing on the three balls (horizontally) you are going to focus on a four "box" zone (horizontally & vertically). For a RH hitter it could be something like B, C, E, & F.

Here's what it would look like with the "Moneyball's."

Ideally, your four box zone will actually overlap boxes and look more like this:

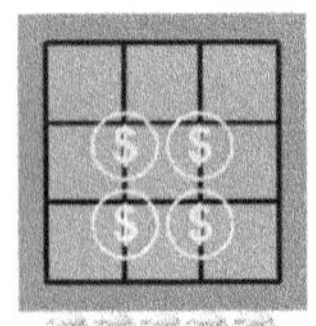

When your focus is here you are looking to drive the ball oppo gap and simply react to an inside fastball where you "turn and burn."

You want to be most aggressive in your zone you're if the count is 0-0, 1-0, 2-0, 3-0, and 3-1. These are hitter's counts for sure. During these counts, you are looking to do the most damage. If you're not sure what your Moneyball zone is, start paying more attention when you hit so you can build more awareness

Even if the count is 0-1, 1-1, or 2-1 you can still be aggressive hunting fastball in your Moneyball zone. Once you get to two strikes you're still timing the fastball in your zone but reacting to off speed and you're able to hit one ball away.

If you really want to be a great hitter, keep a notbook with you for each game. After every at bat, simply mark what zones you swung at and what the counts were when you swung. Review after every single game. This will help you build massive awareness of your hitting.

Don't forget when it's game time, you very well may have to alter your plan based on who is on the mound. For example, if you're facing a pitcher who always throws inside fastballs on 2-0, but your Moneyball zone is middle-away, it would be foolish to let the inside fastball go if you know it's coming. Another example: let's say the count is 2-1, and you're a lefty who is not crazy of the low and away...). However, the pitcher you're facing throws a ++ breaking ball on 2 strikes. You have to ask yourself: "Do I prefer to hit a low and away fastball, or a nasty breaking ball?" If you prefer the low and away fastball, you may need to expand slightly those for just that one pitch. Have a game plan that is built around your strengths and weaknesses. Plan ahead based on the count. Understand that if you're in high school or lower, you will rarely face a pitcher who is spotting his pitches like it's nobody's business. That's more college and pro ball. But, if you're facing a pitcher who has tendencies that go against your original plan, make an adjustment. Compensate and hit. Adapt.

Last piece of advice on this: will this exercise take time? Will it be tedious? Will it require discipline? Yes, yes, and yes. But it comes down to how great you want to be as a hitter. Everyday, hitters say they want to be great. That's great but talk is cheap. I'll believe you when you show me. Don't say it. DO IT." Everyone says they want to be great, but the actions show it. If you say you want to be great, but you find yourself surfing Netflix and playing MLB the Show and Warzone for hours every day, you apparently don't want to be great...you're cool with being just ok. So the choice is yours..what type of hitter do you want to be?

One Drill You Can Do Today: One Zone Tee Drill

Focus on one zone hitting during tee work. Set the tee up in your Moneyball zone and drive it. This drill will help you make purposeful contact with the ball and increase your spread on the field. You can also simulate a pitch over any part of the plate by placing your tee in different zones. Concentrate on sending outside pitches to the opposite field which is more effective than pulling an outside pitch. To work on your opposite field hitting, set up your tee on the back right of the plate if you're a right handed hitter or back left if you're a left handed hitter. This drill will help with your timing and barrel placement on outside pitches, helping you to drive the ball oppo gap.

So there you go. Those are the three biggest mistakes most hitters make and what you can do to avoid them. Yes, there are other mistakes hitters can and do make but correcting these three will eliminate a lot of a hitter's struggles. You would also be surprised by how many mechanical swing

flaws are actually caused by one of these three mindset and approach mistakes.
An easy example is something like this. Your right handed hitting son keeps rolling over to the shortstop. You think it's a mechanical issue so that's how you address it. But in reality he's waiting until he sees the pitch to decide if he's going to swing (passive versus aggressive) so he's actually late and tries to speed up at the last minute. Focus on avoiding these three huge mistakes and you will see much better results.

Pretty much everyone agrees that hitting a baseball is one of the most difficult things to do in sports. Professional hitters only succeed three times out of every ten at-bats, and even the best hitters in history only had a career batting average of around .300. So what separates the successful from the unsuccessful when it comes to hitting? A majority of it has to do with approach and mindset. Major League hitters know that hitting is all about making adjustments, whether it's changing their stance or grip, or altering their swing mechanics. They also know that they will fail more often than they succeed, but they use their failures as opportunities to learn and improve. In other words, they have a major league approach and mindset. If you want to be a successful hitter, you need to adopt the same approach and mindset. Stop thinking about hitting as a binary proposition (either you succeed or you fail). Instead, think of it as a process that you can always be working to improve. Focus on making small adjustments and on using your failures as learning experiences. If you do that, success will eventually come.

Another thing German wanted to Julian to understand is that depending on where he hits in the lineup, there are different expectations. While this year Julian primarily batted clean-up he has hit anywhere from 1-6 in his high school career. In baseball, every player has an important role to play, no matter where they hit in the lineup. The notion that only the "star" players are important is false - every single player on the team is essential to the success of the team. The leadoff hitter sets the tone for the game, and the cleanup hitter needs to drive in runs. The role of the seventh hitter may be different from the role of the second hitter, but both are essential to the success of the team. Every player on a baseball team is important, and each one has a specific role to play. When everyone does their job, the team is successful.

German broke it down like this:

Lead-Off Hitter Notes

You set the tone for the offense!
Main Goal: Get on base and score runs.
Teams that score first have a big advantage!
Early in the game:
Take more pitches. Try and make the pitchers establish a rhythm. Get the starter to a high pitch count.
Expose the pitchers tendencies and inconsistencies as much as possible for yourself and your teammates.
See what type of movement his FB has, as well as the other pitches in his arsenal. Share the info with your teammates.
DO NOT BE AFRAID TO HIT WITH 2 K's!
Always be ready to hit but you need to understand your role and work the pitcher.
You must have a discipline about yourself and what you are trying to achieve.
Do NOT attempt to bunt for a base hit with an 0-1 count
As a lead-off hitter, the game is cut into thirds: 1st 3rd inn. / 4th-6th inn. / 7th-9th inn.
The FB should indicate what type of hit plan you may incorporate for that game.
You don't have to be a passive hitter. The game situation will dictate your approach.
Know the History of the Pitcher
Ball to strike % and BB Ratio
Command of off-speed or certain pitches
Does he have an out pitch?
Slow starter?
A 2-0/3-1 count in some game situations may require you to take a strike to get on base.
Know where you are with your hitting game at certain points of the season to determine your hit plan.
Take advantage of spring training to see a lot of pitches.
You must be a good 2K hitter.
Practice your bunting with great focus.
Be patient with a base stealer on 1B to give him a chance to advance to 2B.

Always study the pitcher; even while on the bench. Find something that you can exploit
Everything that you do, do with great focus!

Middle of the Order Hitters-3, 4, 5, 6

Main Goal: Be a consistent run producer.
Show strike zone discipline, knowing that pitchers are not going to allow you to beat them
Understand pitcher tendencies with runners in scoring position.
Show that you are a consistent threat and tough out in the order.
Understand your role in different situations of the game. Up by runs/Down by runs
Have a disciplined plan throughout the game. Have a plan, work your plan and do not let your plan work you.
Knowing that moving a runner over with a man on 2nd and no outs is not necessary giving yourself up, but still getting the job done.
Be a patient hitter with nobody on. Not going up there with solo homerun mentancy
Understand that I should be a fastball first, type of hitter and adjust from there.
Know the history of the pitcher
Do not be afraid of two strikes. Give up part of the field to allow for better contact.
Be disciplined and focused on your game plans throughout the season.
Know when there is a good time to drive the ball versus taking what the pitcher gives you.
Understand how to get runners in from 3rd base consistently
Stay through the middle of the field
Look for ball up in the zone with the infield in (Look for pitch to drive; on the beltline)
Understand the pitcher's out pitch and how he sets you up for that pitch
Keep your batting practice and pre-game routine consistent.
Mentally stay focused and trust yourself in RBI situations. Know that you are going to get the job done.
Pressure is on the pitcher with runners on. Do not allow the pressure to succeed, to affect your plan.

If you're serious about baseball and want to play at the next level, then you know that hitting is the key to success. It's the one consistent thing that major league teams look for when evaluating players. So, if you want to stand out from the crowd and give yourself a leg up on the competition, then it's time to start thinking like a major league hitter. Like they say, "If you hit, you don't sit."

The first thing you need to understand is that hitting is all about consistency. Major league hitters are able to consistently make hard contact with the ball because they have a clear understanding of their swing and they keep their mechanics in check. They also have a good feel for the strike zone and they know how to work counts in their favor. As a result, they very rarely get fooled by pitches or make weak contact.

Of course, consistency is only half the battle. The other half is having the right approach at the plate. Major league hitters know how to situationally hit and they're always looking for ways to put themselves in a position to succeed. They're willing to take walks when necessary and they're not afraid to hit with two strikes. They also have a knack for coming up with big hits in clutch situations.

Most players know that hitting is the key to success on the diamond. But what many don't realize is that at least 80% of hitting is mindset and approach, while only 20% is mechanics. The best hitters in the game have a positive mindset and approach their at-bats with confidence. They know their strengths and adjust their approach accordingly. They also have a short memory, so they don't let past failures affect their current at-bat. Instead, they focus on making good contact and letting the results take care of themselves. While proper mechanics are important, it's the mindset and approach that separates the best hitters from the rest. So if you want to improve your hitting, start by working on your mindset and approach. The results will follow.

About German & Bobby's

German Duran

Germán Durán was a Major League Baseball player for the Texas Rangers (2008). Duran was born in Zacatecas, Mexico, raised in Fort Worth, Texas, and drafted in 2003 by the Cincinnati Reds, out of Paschal High School (Fort Worth, TX).

German Duran chose not to sign, went on to Texas Christian University, where he posted a .330/.427/.492 slash line, a Collegiate Baseball All-American his freshman year at TCU. He then transferred to Weatherford College, where he was drafted again, this time in the sixth round of the 2005 Baseball Draft, by a scout named Jay Eddings, beginning his professional baseball career.

Duran progressed through the minor league system systematically, moving from A- ball in 2005 (Spokane Indians), to A+ in 2006 (Bakersfield Blaze), to Double-A in 2007 (Frisco RoughRigers), and on to Triple-A in 2008 (Oklahoma RedHawks), before being called-up to the Rangers in April 2008 to replace an injured Hank Blalock.

On April 17, 2008, Durán made his major league debut against the Toronto Blue Jays. He hit his first home run on May 4, 2008, versus the Oakland Athletics. Duran was placed on waivers by the Rangers on June 26, 2009, and was claimed by the Houston Astros on July 1, 2009.

German Duran played in the Mexican Baseball league in 2011 before joining the Grand Prairie AirHogs of the American Association. Hitting .317 in 12 games near the end of the season, Duran then hit .536 with 10 RBI in the playoffs, including a home run in game five of the championship series as the AirHogs won the championship over the St. Paul Saints. In December, the AirHogs sold his contract to the Miami Marlins.

Bobby Minor

As a player Bobby played D1 college baseball at Prairie View A&M before an arm injury cut his collegiate career short. He later played on a men's travel team playing in Mexico several times. He is also a former high school baseball coach and previously founded a select baseball club in DFW. Bobby has extensive player development and coaching experience at multiple levels. He also worked with the son of a MLB HOF'r running an event in the Dominican Republic for four years. Currently, he enjoys being a parent and coach to son Julian and watching him as he navigates the college recruiting process. As 15 year old Julian played for the 15U Team Puerto Rico in the "World Comes to the Palm Beaches" West Palm Beach, Florida and in January 2020 was one of 80 high school players selected for the 2020 MLB Dream Series in Tempe, AZ. Bobby brings a unique combination of skills and experience to the team in that, while he has over 25 years of sales and marketing experience with several Fortune 500 companies, he's also a baseball guy.

As if all of the incredible content German provided in this book wasn't enough, I asked him what else could he share that he thought would help hitters think like a Major League Hitter and take their game to the next level.

Here's what he shared with me:

****Bonus #1: 7 Situational Stations for a Hitter's In-Game Preparation**

If most average to below average hitters are honest the only place they prepare is in the on-deck circle. That's why they aren't elite level hitters. Elite level hitters know they have seven, count them, seven opportunities to prepare during the game. German said that was one the things that made him different. He was always working, always studying, always asking questions (to guys like Michael Young and Josh Hamilton, guys that know a little bit about hitting...), always looking for an edge or advantage.

He said **the first place he prepares is in the dugout before an at-bat**. While other guys are joking around, checking their phone, anything and everything but focusing on the game, German was locked in and using this opportunity to prepare. What was he looking for? The opposing pitcher's tendencies: Did he have a tendency to throw a particular pitch in a situation? Did he have a tendency to throw a particular pitch in a particular count? What were his go-to pitches, did he start most batter's off with a fastball? Did he usually throw a curve in the dirt when he was up 0-2? Did he tend to throw the same pitch or do the same thing in similar situations? Notice his release point - did he change it and when? Does he come more over the top on a particular pitch? Does his arm slot change? Does he do anything different when the ball is in his glove? What are his strengths and apparent weaknesses. Can he locate his fastball? Does he struggle to throw his off-speed for a strike? Which pitch is he most comfortable throwing? Which pitch is he avoiding? He would also watch how his teammates handled the pitcher. Were they late on his fastball? Did they have trouble picking up the ball out of his hand? Was there anything the pitcher did to disrupt their timing.

The next place he would prepare is in the on deck circle. Most hitters think this is simply the place you get loose before stepping up to the plate but it's way more than that. This is where you take practice swings, continue to time the pitcher, and review the mental keys you use: line-drive the other way, stay balanced, etc.

In route to the batter's box is one of the most overlooked places a hitter can prepare. As you're walking up to the plate you should be assessing the game situation. Is there a runner on 3B, 2B, 1B? Do you want to move the runner over? What location & what pitch are you looking for? Are you working three balls in the middle looking for a fastball? Are you looking for something middle away so you can hit behind the runner? Are you looking for something up you can hit in the air so the runner can tag? Have you plan formulated before you reach the box? You have to have a plan you are striving to execute.

Outside the batter's box (Before stepping in) is the next station for in-game preparation.
Here's where you really lock in. Give yourself one more reminder of your mechanical cue whatever that might be. Maybe it's "stay back", "keep my hands inside the ball", "see it deep", anything like that. Next take a deep breath - breath in slowly and exhale. You're letting the carbon dioxide (reducing the muscle inhibition) out and keeping oxygen in (the muscle enhancer remains). Now, relax.

As you step into the batter's box this is your next station for in-game preparation. Get into the box with a clear head. The only message you should hear from your self-talk should be "See the ball." Be easy and be ready. A lot of hitters tense up when they get in the box because they are usually "outcome focused" (which you can't control) instead of being "process focused" (where you know you're prepared) because they've wasted four other opportunities to get prepared before they get here. If you're thinking about mechanics or anything else call time and get out of the box. Clear your head, take a deep breath and relax.

Whether it's before you see a pitch, after you take a pitch, swing and miss, or foul a pitch off, **the next station for in-game preparation is outside the box.** If you are not 100% locked-in and focused step out of the box and fix your thinking pattern. It's ok, it happens. But then coach yourself with positive self-talk or a simple reminder like, "Just see the ball." Take another deep breath. If all is well, tell yourself, "Stay right there".

The last and final station for in-game preparation is again back in the dugout but this time after an at-bat. Take a minute and review your at-bat. If you keep a hitting journal or take in-game notes write things down while they're fresh in your mind. Be brutally honest with yourself but don't beat yourself up. If you're satisfied with your approach, irrespective of the result, then leave it alone. Remember focus on the process not the outcome. Over the course of a season you will have several balls you barrel but they straight to someone and several you miss but the drop in or find a hole. It evens out. Keep that in mind. If you're unhappy with it ask these questions: What was I trying to do? What went wrong? & What do I want to do next time? Recognize what you did wrong and then flush it. Play a mental movie in your head where you execute the way you wanted. Then ask yourself what can I share with my teammates to help them from what I've learned. Maybe you saw the pitcher tip his pitches, maybe it was something else. Whatever it is share it with them to help them better prepare. After that leave it alone and get your head back into the game.

Doing these things consistently will change you as a hitter without making any changes to your swing.

****Bonus #2: "5 Parts of the Swing" Hitting Checklist**

1. Launch Position

While you can have 100 different batters have 100 different stances and starts to their swing, the launch position is a critical starting point for a successful baseball swing and where most great hitters all look alike. From here, the batter can generate the power needed to drive the ball. To get into the launch position, the front foot should be turned at a 45 degree angle, with the hands over the back toes. The bat should be cocked at an angle, and the belly button should be pulled in. There should be flexion in the front elbow, and the back elbow should be turned at a 45 degree angle. The chin should be in front of the shoulder. By following these steps, the batter will be in a strong position to hitting the ball.

- ☑ Front foot 45 degrees
- ☑ Hands over back toes
- ☑ Bat angle - cock
- ☑ Belly button in
- ☑ Flexion front elbow
- ☑ Back elbow 45 degrees
- ☑ Chin front shoulder

2. Initiating the Swing

One of the most important aspects of hitting a baseball is initiating the swing. There are a few key elements to keep in mind when doing this. First, the back foot should rotate so that the toes point outward. This will help to create a strong base for the rest of the swing. Next, the lead hip should open slightly. This will help to generate power from the lower body. The front shoulder should remain closed during the swing, and the rear elbow should be at a 90-degree angle. The hands should be equal to or in front of the elbow, and they should be inside the baseball. These elements are all important in creating a powerful and accurate swing.

- ☑ Back foot rotates
- ☑ Lead hip opens
- ☑ Front shoulder closed
- ☑ Rear elbow 90 degrees
- ☑ Hands equal to or in front of elbow
- ☑ Hands inside baseball

3. Contact

The contact position in a baseball swing is the position of the hitter's body just before making contact with the ball. The ideal contact position will vary depending on the hitter's individual hitting style, but there are some general guidelines that all hitters should follow. The back leg should be positioned slightly behind the front leg, and the lower body should be thrust forward. The bellybutton should be lined up with the pitcher, and the front leg should be kept stiff. The top hand should be up, and the bottom hand should be down. The hands should be across the chest, and the elbows should be tucked in. Following these guidelines will help to ensure that the hitter makes solid contact with the ball.

- ☑ L-back leg
- ☑ Lower body thrust forward
- ☑ Bellybutton pitcher
- ☑ Front leg stiff
- ☑ Top hand up
- ☑ Bottom hand down
- ☑ Hands across the chest

4. Extension

One of the key elements of a good swing is extension, or the process of fully extending the arms and bat through the hitting zone. This adds power to the swing and increases the chances of making solid contact with the ball. To achieve proper extension, a batter must keep their hands over their front toe as they swing. Additionally, their front foot should be at a 90-degree angle, and their back leg should remain in an L-position. Finally, the batter's head should be down so that they can see the barrel of the bat as they make contact with the ball. By following these simple guidelines, hitters can increase their chances of hitting the ball hard and putting it into play.

- ☑ After contact
- ☑ Hands over front toe
- ☑ Front foot 90 degrees
- ☑ L-position remains
- ☑ Head down barrel of bat

5. Follow Through

One of the most important aspects of hitting a baseball is follow through. After making contact with the ball, it is important to keep your hands over your back toes and finish the swing outside of your shoulder. Your back shoulder should be facing the pitcher when you finish the swing. This will ensure that you generate maximum power and accuracy. By following these simple tips, you can improve your hitting and give yourself a better chance of success at the plate.

- ☑ Hands over back toes
- ☑ Outside the shoulder
- ☑ Back shoulder facing pitcher

Bonus #3: Mastering Two-Strike Hitting

German is huge on being a good two-strike hitter. The major league average of all at bats with 2 strikes is 48%. What does that say about 2 strike hitting? Traditionally hitters have been taught to change their swing. Suggestions such as choking up, widening their stance, no stride, moving close to the plate or crouching down to make their strike zone smaller are common. If a hitter thinks this helps, so be it. I do believe that choking up will give you better control; it is just common sense. However, the real problem is the mind (approach - plan - mental toughness).
So what will that be at the AAA - AA - A - or rookie level be?

So everybody says we have to have a good 2 strike approach. Let's look at this for a minute.
DNA Chart over the last 5 years:
0-2 = .168
1-2 = .182
2-2 = .195
3-2 = .233

People have been trying for years to answer this problem. How can we hit for a better average with 2 strikes? Let's be honest, we are not going to start hitting .300 with 2 strikes because of some new stance. What we can do is be more productive with 2 strikes. Put the ball in play, while you still made an out, you did not strikeout. Some of you may have moved a runner, had an 8 pitch or more AB, been a tough out, or made the pitcher work to get you out. In other words you helped your team even with 2 strikes. We will not see a big rise in our average with 2 strikes but we should see productive ABs rise as a result.

Approach

The hitter must be able to stay square and back the ball up to use the whole field. If you can't hit the ball the other way, you will never be a good situational hitter and you will never have a good 2 strike approach. It is as simple as that. So the hitter that tries to pull the ball, with a pull approach has no chance. What we see is the hitter leaking on the front side (hip - shoulder - etc.). The cast of the hands - pull swing. So while we should work very hard on cleaning up the hitters mechanics, we must also concentrate on the mind - approach - plan. Mentally we can help our mechanics. By thinking opposite gap - I'm taking every FB the other way - no matter where it is. By never getting off the FB timing wise and thinking I'm taking every FB the other way (even the inside FB), then the hitter will have a chance to be on the off speed pitch.

Widen your strike zone with 2 strikes - I DON'T THINK SO- Work off 3 balls in the middle. Look 1 ball off center, so when we look away, just look 1 ball. You will be able to handle 6 more inches away easy and that will cover the plate but if you start looking on the corner (the black) you will chase balls off the plate. So be careful how you approach strike zone management.

So change your thinking. The mind should be convinced that it has complete control of the situation - Confidence. Look to hit the ball in the opposite field gap.

It's amazing what 2 strikes can do to a hitter; if the hitter allows it.

Chasing a pitch over your head or a pitch bouncing in the dirt with 2 strikes comes from either a fear of striking out or complete lack of concentration. If you do strikeout on a bastard pitch, tip your hat but tell yourself that he can't and won't do that again.

You will be successful with 2 strikes if you have a clear, confident mind. Stay square – back the ball up - commit to take every FB the other way and compete.

Hitters must realize that it takes only one strike to hit a single, double, triple or homerun. Successful hitting can come on the first strike, second strike or the third strike. So if it takes only one strike to help your team win, the fact is every strike is important and of equal importance. The third strike has no more importance than the first two unless you give it more. If the hitter fears striking out, he had better change professions, because striking out is inevitable. It happens to the best in the game. The hitter should know that when they fear striking out, they are increasing the skill level of the pitcher and in doing so, giving him the competitive edge. The hitter must use the same mental approach no matter what the count is.

Why!? Why do some hitters seem to hit with 2 strikes much more than the 48% average? This must be addressed. Answer this question: It can't just be have a good 2 strike approach but why are you hitting with 2 strikes all the time? Pitch recognition is usually a big part of the problem with timing being the culprit. You have ¼ second to decide what the pitch is and location. If you are late with your timing your are in trouble. A catch-up swing is always a pull swing - around the ball swing - working off the ball – collision swing - you get the point. Poor decisions are made on strike zone management. So I know you will work hard on the hitter's mechanics and you should. However, don't confuse mechanics and timing. They are 2 different problems but sometimes lead us to talk about symptoms instead of the true problem. See separation - pitch recognition - located under symptoms in this handout.

Physical Change - Better Bat Control Mentally - Never get off the FB with your timing You must never guess what a pitchers out pitch might be. However, if you have done your homework on the pitcher and you are very sure of what his go to pitch is on the third strike, you can anticipate that pitch with FB timing. Remember, being very sure does not mean guessing. Informed anticipation is developed by past history with a particular pitcher and by watching the pitcher during the game to see if there is any change in his pitch pattern. Think Hit Every FB the Other Way -- This will keep you on the off speed stuff Commit to the opposite field gap or the off field. When You Look Away - Just 1 ball off center Don't be Late - If you make a mistake, be early You Must Put the Ball In Play Compete - Have some guts

*This is personal! Don't get off the fastball with your timing and react to the other pitches. There is no pressure on the defense when the pitcher records a strikeout. Do not become a defensive hitter. You must maintain confidence in your abilities with 2 strikes. This is just another offensive challenge.

Bonus #4: "Perfect Timing" Cheat Sheet

Good timing means getting the body into a strong position so that when the stride foot lands, the ball is still far enough away. This allows the hitter to take his best swing at any pitch, at any velocity. A good hitter times the pitch, putting his body in the right place at the right time.

Timing and rhythm are crucial. You must be in a good balanced position to hit while the pitch is still far enough away for you to recognize it. Whatever kind of trigger you use: tap, kick, or stride. You have to start it early enough to give yourself as much time as possible to see the pitch. You must land on the balls of your feet at the correct time - when the ball is still about halfway to home plate - to give yourself as much time as possible to recognize the pitch.

When a hitter takes his stride and his front foot lands on the ground, the ball should be halfway between the mound and home plate or just a little past halfway. The problem is the hitter can't tell exactly where the halfway point is, but he does know that the ball isn't on top of him and he does know the pitcher doesn't still have the ball in his hand. The ball is moving toward home plate. Now all the hitter has to do is recognize the pitch and begin a good, aggressive swing.

A hitter may not see the ball correctly if he's late or feels everything is rushed. When hitters learn that timing is just putting the body in the right place at the right time, the ball will look bigger and the pitch will seem slower.

You cannot increase bat speed or swing harder to catch up to a fastball. Your bat speed is not going to change from pitch to pitch. What you can change, however, is your timing. When facing a hard thrower, don't try to swing harder. Start your rhythm and timing sooner and the bat will have a chance to get to the ball on time. Begin a motion that will set up your swing. It doesn't mean you should commit early by bringing the bat head around or start the swing itself early. You must get your front foot down before the swing begins and early motion allows you to separate to balance and be on time.

Dancing with the Pitcher

Timing is really dancing with the pitcher because you must react to his movements. A hitter must put himself in the right position at the right time.

Early timing is better than late timing. If a hitter starts a little too early, he can always slow down and be right on any pitch he recognizes correctly. On the other hand, if a hitter starts too late he cannot make up lost time and will probably rush or jump at the ball.

Once in motion, the hitter's eyes will tell him when and where to deliver the bat. If the hitter starts his ready motion late, he cuts down the time his eyes have to make a good judgment on where and when to deliver the bat and ends up using a very rushed movement.

To time a pitcher, a hitter must trust his eyes, know, and feel what he's looking at when he steps into the batter's box. After a pitch or two, a hitter should know if he's close to being on time or if he's too late or too early. It does not matter what pitch the pitcher throws because a hitter must always be on time for the pitcher's fastball. Once the ball is released, a hitter who is on time for the pitcher's fastball can make an adjustment to an off-speed pitch by simply slowing down for a split second and letting the ball travel to the hitting zone somewhere over the plate.

For a hitter, good rhythm and timing require moving in relation to the pitcher's motions. Most of the time, you want to start moving when the pitcher breaks his hands. Whether the pitcher works from the windup or the stretch, he will have to break his hands. He can't fool you. What you're doing is dancing with the pitcher.

When the pitcher breaks his hands, the hitter must maintain his posture and stride on time, landing on the inside of the balls of his feet. The front foot can land open, at almost a 45-degree angle. A hitter should not land on his heels.

Good hitters start early and slow while maintaining a fluid motion. Just keep the motion going until your stride foot lands on the ground. You cannot get aggressive until your foot lands. Many hitters try to get aggressive before they land, turning their approach into a jump or lunge.

Starting your motion early is better than starting large. When a hitter starts early, it's much easier for him to adjust. A hitter can always slow down. A hitter who starts late can never catch up. If you start your motion too early, just say to yourself, “oh no, this is too soon,” and slow everything down to a fluid movement. Don't stop. If you stop, you'll have to restart.

Hitters who chased bad pitches were often told to see the ball first, and then react. This old teaching doesn't work. The big problem with this idea is that the hitter will run out of time. The two-tenths of a second the hitter has to make a good decision will be gone.

Seeing the ball is a good idea, the hitter must see the ball while he's in motion or while he's getting ready to attack. The hitter starting early means that the hitter's body is in motion and is set up to hit the pitch before the pitcher gets to his release point.

Don't be afraid of movement. Timing requires movement. The swing requires movement. Everything about hitting consists of good, fluid movements.

www.ingramcontent.com/pod-product-compliance
Lightning Source LLC
LaVergne TN
LVHW082259150826
845677LV00009B/1665
* 9 7 9 8 8 4 4 0 6 5 6 6 8 *